Ugh, Life!

OKUHLE ESETHU

OE PUBLICATIONS

First published in South Africa in 2023 by

OE Publications

Copyright © Lindokuhle Esethu Hlatshwayo, 2023

ISBN: 978-0-6397-9588-1

For more information visit: www.oepublications.com

GRATITUDE

Becoming A Writer. My Teenage Years. Poetry.

I wake up before 5 AM to write every morning.

When I am home, she always makes sure that there is coffee or hot chocolate in the house, even though I am the only one who consumes caffeine. She bakes for me so that I can have my coffee or hot chocolate with some banana loaf or cookies—my favourites.

Those small gestures of love, which keep me inspired and provide warmth for my heart in the morning, mean the world to me.

Mama!

Thank you for my life and for supporting my dreams.

xx

To my late stepfather, whom I called "Bhut'Hlabi"

My mind wrestles with this word, "Gone." How is it that I will never see you again!? I still have too many *Thank You's* to give you.

My teenage memories are filled with love, warmth and buckets of laughter because of you.

The memories are there as proof of the fatherly love you poured into us, Nhlanhla and I. Love that shocked the whole world as they witnessed a man wholeheartedly love children that were not biologically his. Everyone who visited our home saw your love in your gestures. They heard it in your warm and loving voice and felt it in every corner of the house. You were the hearth fire that brought warmth into our lives. Your presence in my life erased the parts of me that desperately wanted to be seen by the world; I felt loved, seen and heard at home. You directed me to my passion and dreams by encouraging me to give everything that piqued my interest a try until I found one that hit home. I have! Hence, I am writing this book now. How I wish you were here for this moment!

God knew I'd need a father like you to become the woman I am today. I am so grateful to have crossed paths with you.

Ngibonga uthando lwakho, **Hlabeyakhe Maxwell Mbukwame**.

xx

To Quaz Roodt, my poetry teacher from UJ Arts & Culture Academy.

Thank you for sharing your love and passion for poetry with us, UJ Poets.

Thank you for helping me find my writing voice and for teaching me how to give expression and form to my thoughts and emotions through poetry. The two years I spent under your wings gave me the courage to soar high in the world of literature and storytelling.

I will forever appreciate you.

God bless you.

♥

Lindokuhle Esethu Hlatshwayo

CONTENTS

Poetry I wrote as a teenager.

*When I was putting these words together, I didn't think
that it was poetry I was writing, at first.*

*My body was erupting with volcanic teenage
emotions, thoughts, and hormones
that screamed at me to give them
expression and form.
So, I picked up my pen.*

*These are words that held my life together
as a teenager.*

LIVING

PART 1: LIVING

Purpose

Self-Doubt

Fear

Forefathers

Learning

Writing

Dreaming

Poetry

Self-Discovery

HeART

Time

Passion

Childhood

July

Writing From The Heart

As soon as I held my pen,
words ceased to flow
from my mind
to the page in front of me.

Not because I had forgotten
how to put them together,
but because I wrote
from my mind,
not my heart.

I wrote what I thought
the world would like to read,
not my truth.

I was caged all over again.
I had to try to find a way back to myself…

Purpose

with nothing to live for,
the banality of my life
has become a bore,
even to me.

the mere thought of living exhausts me.

The Poetry Of Life

TO THE DEPRESSED, HALF-ALIVE, PART OF ME

READ THIS OUT LOUD WHEN YOU FEEL LIKE
LIFE IS NOT WORTH LIVING.

I am going to be enchanted by sunrises, again.
I am going to love the richness of coffee
dancing on my tongue in the morning, again.
I am going to look forward to meeting new people
and discovering new worlds, again.
I am going to sing along to and dance
to my favourite songs, again.
I am going to laugh from the belly, again.
I am going to feel at peace when I stargaze at night
or cloud-gaze during the day, again.
I am going to feel calm when birds chirp
graciously outside my window, again.
I am going to enjoy getting lost in the pages of
good books, again.
I am going to look forward to waking up, again.
I am going to dream, again.

Okuhle Esethu

I am going to want to make a difference,
to inspire others, again.
I am going to want to be kinder, better,
and more loving, again.
I am going to be fascinated by the talented writers,
poets, and artists, again.
I am going to love writing and reciting poetry, again.
I am going to enjoy dressing up and going out
with my friends, again.
I am going to smile and be happy, again.
I am going to thank God for life, again.
I am going to rediscover myself, again.
I am going to fall in love with life, again.
I am going to want to live
because I am going to see the magic of life, again.

SIT IN YOUR PAIN, IT GETS BETTER.

Promises Of Life

without any promises that life will get better

or obligations for it to become easier for me,

something is whispering inside me,

to me,

telling me to keep fighting,

to push through the days that seem devoid of meaning,

to not end it…

July

the bad days are longer, darker
than the good days.

melancholy is louder, much stronger
than joy.

each day erodes life from my soul.
i've become an empty cup.

i hope i make it. i really hope i can make it
to july, at least.

Wings

If I had to pick a superpower,
I'd pick wings,
and fly away.

To experience what it is like to be in heaven,
in love with life,
truly alive.

To see the world from God's point of view,
away from the noise
made by loveless crowds.

A Caterpillar

today,
i am a butterfly.
but i wish i had stayed a caterpillar for longer.
my wings are caged
by fear, anxiety, and self-doubt.

the universe says i am ready to fly
and share my beauty with the world,
so does my heart.

with so many other butterflies out there,
does it matter if i fly
or stay where i am safe?

My House! My Rules!

self doubt,
like the full moon,
graces everyone with his presence
from time to time.

shut all your windows!
keep his fatal lustre out.
draw the line and put him in his place.

Doubt, The Skank

Doubt, the skank.
The best prostitute in town.
Seductive in nature.
Not that expensive—just a rand and a man's greatness.

She skilfully spreads her legs
inside her host's mind,
hardens his ego,
and shrinks his flair into mediocrity.

Doubt, the skank.
Every lame man's dirty secret.
Deft at seducing imaginative minds
into dumbwits who fear their dreams
more than disease and dying with potential.

Casket Dreams

i've wasted the finest days of my life,
drowning and losing myself
in the shallow pool of procrastination.

confined in the illusion of life's grace period,
letting my prime years
erode into skeletons of an unfulfilling life.

i watched my childhood dreams die
and rot under the coarse soils of self-sabotage,
inside caskets carved from confusion and distraction.

Fear

fear is vile.
it kills desire
in silence.

it is seductive in nature.
it introduces itself as a friend
before carrying out the assassination of one's dreams.

Our Forefathers

We wouldn't be so scared of our dreams,
so passive,
if we remembered that our forefathers
awaited and dreamed of
a bright future for this nation.

A future with us.
A future where we were the future.

We wouldn't be so scared of ourselves,
so reckless,
if we realised that the future our forefathers
waited for and dreamed of
is now here.

Living For Our Ancestors

we scratched beyond the surface.
we dug deep within ourselves.
our search exposed us to old wounds.

we thought we'd find peace after the search,
but the bones of our silenced ancestors
were stuffed with their untold stories.

history bled on us.
so, we took it upon ourselves to bleed on paper,
to heal our ancestors.

You Are A Writer, Write!

Write until your pen bleeds!
Write until your hands go numb!

Stop hiding behind metaphors!
Start telling your truth!

Alive

To be alive
is to be in perpetual evolution,
embracing every revelation,
becoming a revolution.

Human

i've forgotten
how to be human.

to slow down
and breathe.

to sleep. to eat. to laugh. to love.
without feeling guilty.

i've forgotten
how to be here.

to not travel there.
to places not yet here.

Peace

i've never been to the beach,
but i hear people find their true selves there.

peace resides inside the tides.
love floats in the balmy ocean air.
appreciation for life can be gathered, in buckets,
from the tan-coloured, moist sand.

i imagine myself at the beach sometimes,
my feet buried in the sand,
waiting for the waves of the ocean
to knock down the walls
i've built around my heart
and drown my fears.

i yearn to be at the beach most days,
basking in the sun,
with songs of seashells soothing my strained soul.
i just want to know what it feels like to be alive.

Alone

Make time to tend to your soul.

When you are alone,
you dive into the crevices of yourself
you did not know existed before.

A Child Again

Remember how you loved life as a child?
Remember how you danced and laughed
like there was no tomorrow?

The only moment that mattered
was the one you existed in.

Remember how you followed your heart as a child?
Remember how you immersed yourself
in your passions?

Remember how you lived from a place of abundance
and joy as a child?

Remember how you had wings and fluttered in peace
even when your friends walked?

You only did what felt right for your soul.

Remember, and be a child, again!

The Pangs Of Growth

We quickly grew weary playing
in the glittering rays of the sun.
Bored and impatient,
we could not wait to grow up.

We squandered our childhood,
rushing toward the future,
not realising that the future
we looked forward to
could only be brilliant
if we made the present colourful.

We grieved the present
on days we should have been grateful,
not realising that we were living
in our answered prayers each time.
Every moment was the future
we once looked forward to.

Okuhle Esethu

We grew up
and brutally learned
that there never was a future.
Focusing on the future
only stole from the present moment.

We grew up
only to discover that the future
was always hidden in how we lived each day,
in the present moment.

We grew up
and discovered the folly of fixating on the future.
By anticipating what was ahead,
we denied ourselves the blessing of truly living
in the present moment.

Growth

Growth is a dance.
Not a light switch.

You'll fall,
lose the rhythm and forget your steps.

But continue dancing, dear child.
You'll get the hang of it eventually.

Childhood

They postponed living...

It had not dawned on them
that they would soon lose
the innocence of their childishness.

Best friends would grow apart.
Passionate lovers would become strangers.

Childhood spared them the misery of life.
Adulthood never announced itself;
it entered their bodies without warning.

Life

Life is fleeting,
like the rays of the sun
glittering
against the curtained windows
of my old neighbour's house.

The Present Moment

Don't wish this moment away.
Don't waste time and your precious life
Looking forward to the better moments of life.
Focus on making a great memory of this moment.

Time

time is poison.

it changes nature and disrupts the routine of life.

time does not move on the whims of men.

it only spoils life.

it corrupts the world.

i am older now

than i was a minute ago.

with each breath i take, i get closer to my last breath.

i do not know whether i should celebrate or mourn

the nearing of my death.

In The Next Life

maybe,
in the next life,
i'll fall in love
with people and things that give me life.

Dear Life

Dear life,

I suddenly look forward to
what you have in store for me.

Today,
I got soaked in the rain.
I danced to the songs of raindrops kissing my skin.
I remembered what it feels like to be alive.

Happiness

life is held together by the small things.
the small moments of life,
put together,
make up the whole thing :)

i'm learning that to be happy with my life,
i have to love the small moments of each day—

a cup of coffee in the morning.
sunrises.
ice-cream.
long walks.
a good book.
fresh flowers in my room.

...small things. small things...

Opening Up To Life

I like the sound of the waves
Crashing against the walls
I've built around my heart,
Opening me up to life,
Sweeping me off my feet
To offer me to a new beginning.

A life filled with love
From God,
From the ocean,
From the true nature of my heart,
From the depths of my soul.

Transforming my being,
Redefining my existence.

Capturing The Moment

some places are so sacred,

some moments so glorious,

that capturing them would be a crime.

the digital world would only taint them.

those places,

those moments,

are meant to be stored in memory,

held in the heart and appreciated from there.

Flow

I am
walking into a lush landscape of pure joy and fulfilment,
letting go of control and going with the flow,
freeing myself from the prison of worry and regret.

I am
ending my detrimental relationship with pessimism
and marrying myself to optimism.

I am
becoming present to the present moment.

I am
taking life's hand and allowing her to guide me,
for who better knows how to create a magical life
for me than life itself?

I am
allowing life to happen for me and never to me,
trusting with my heart, soul, and whole being.
Life loves me.

This Is Life!

On the days when I immerse myself
in the world of literature,

time   dis   appears…

single

moments

become

lifetimes

HeART

you are not alive
until you've fallen in love,
more than once,
with the same thing.

something that makes you look forward to living,
to waking up every morning,
to falling in love with it,
over and over again.

Because Of Poetry, I AM

Poetry,

a sanctuary

where I can heal the broken pieces of myself.

Poetry,

a confessional

where I can tell my truth

and reveal glimpses of myself to myself.

Poetry,

a chapel

where I can be myself

while striving to become a better version of myself.

The Poet's Poem

a poet should live life refining her poem—

constantly
carving and crafting,
writing and rewriting,
redefining herself,
balancing her stanzas,
removing weeds from her words,
sprinkling each line of every day
with synonyms of growth and love.

a poet should strive to be a better poem
every second of her poetic life.

Okuhle Esethu

An Artist Again

In my next life,
I would like to be an artist again.

***Creator and destroyer of worlds.
***Mother of villains and heroes.
***A bartender who joyfully mixes cocktails
of different characters together
to produce explosive yarns.
***A talented magician that can pull hidden emotions
from top hats with words.
***A composer that can create life from nothingness.
***A god that fabricates light from darkness.

I AM

I AM
while I write.
As I write,
I become.

Once it is written and done,
I am no longer what I once was.
Therefore, I cannot claim my art
as mine,
or as a direct reflection of me.

A Lily Flower

and just like a lily,
she appears cocooned and simple at first sight.

but, with time,
she opens up, revealing her magic.

she blooms with divinity,
fertile with creative and enchanting ideas
that have the power to heal the world.

A Butterfly

"How can a once-simple girl embody so much beauty and artistic magic?"

Time.

Okuhle Esethu

Pose Like A Butterfly

Being yourself
looks like dancing out of tune
with the rest of the world,
with no music playing in the real world,
but the song in your heart—
the only sound that matters.

Being yourself
looks like assuming the pose of a butterfly:
wings spread wide open with courage,
not afraid to soar in your dreams.

Death

If you were told that you were going to die tomorrow,
then you'd live.

You'd smell and savour the richness of your coffee.
You'd really taste your food when you eat.
You'd bask in the sun and dance in the rain.
You'd forgive yourself.
You'd tell your truth.
You'd only do the things you love.
You'd look at the faces of your loved ones
when you talk to them.
You'd follow your heart.
Your hugs would be warm and longer.

Live!
You are going to die, tomorrow.

GRIEVING

PART 2: GRIEVING

1. Grief.
2. Pus.
3. Grieving Like A Mad Man.
4. Dad.
5. Inheriting My Father's Hands.
6. Your Departure.
7. Far Away.
8. Second Chances.
9. Going Back Home.
10. Ex.
11. Poems I Wrote For You While You Were Gone.
12. I Love You.
13. Dear Love.
14. Heartbreak.
15. Healing Bruises.
16. How To Deal With A Heartbreak.
17. Experiences.
18. Tug-of-War.
19. Scattered Iterations of Life.
20. The Past.
21. A Heavenly Letter.
22. Mourning Shadows.
23. Uninvited Visitor.
24. Childhood Museum.

Old Self

Mourning

Memories

Dad

Father Figure

Heartbreak

Violence

Home

Gogo

Love

Forgiveness

Second Chances

Experiences

Old Bonds

The Past

Grief

run away!
hide!
in the darkest crevices and corners
of your traumatised mind.

to lick those wounds.
to grieve the parts of yourself
you lost
loving them.

Pus

so dense
the grief
in your heart,
it shows up in your body
and oozes through your pores.

Grieving Like A Madman

tear my skin and limbs into timbers

to create a bonfire

to warm my heart

to wake your cold body

and give us a proper goodbye.

Dad

Every time I go home to see my dad,
I find him wearing the warmest smile on his face,
his eyes glistening with pride.

Our conversations are forever animated;
I leave feeling loved and inspired.

Inheriting My Father's Hands

My father was a man!
A man who never showed emotion,
unless it was anger.
He loved my mother with clenched fists
instead of open arms.
His sooty, heavy hands
carried and cared for life
but could also end a life.
He hid quiet riots in his palms
while his violent tantrums
hissed to be born.

My father was a man!
A stone-hearted lover.
A devastated, scared little boy
who camouflaged his fear as manliness.
He wore his childhood bruises
on his wrists like tattoos.
His scars were remnants of his sorrow.

Okuhle Esethu

My father was a man!
My father was an angry man.
Angry men bleed the most.
They weigh down those they love
with the weight of their manliness
and their empty worlds.

My father was a man!
He made sure that we suffered
the sins of his past.
He turned our home into a slaughterhouse
and made love to my mother
with knuckles divorced from peace.

My father was a man!
He carried earthquakes in his hands.
A faint of death drew lines on his wrists.
A flavour of mortality formed around his knuckles.
With fists, he threw fits of rage.
His possessed hands played God
And turned my mother into a memory,
her flesh into a grave.

Ugh, Life!

My father was a scared and broken little boy
whose father was a man.
Today, I am a scared and broken little boy,
but perhaps I shall inherit
my father's hands someday.
With fists,
I will pass down my trauma
and become a man,
like my father.

Your Departure

after an entire year,
yesterday i finally mourned your departure.
when i peeped into your empty wardrobe,
a wave of sadness swept away
the sandcastle of joys and hopes
i had built for our family.

you are not my father anymore.
i am not your daughter.
we are only akin by memories.

the smell of tea in the evening reminds me of you.
flipping through channels for the perfect movie
after dinner is unexciting.
your couch is cold and unoccupied.
mom does not cook anymore;
we live off takeaways
as if you took away
her stove,
her pots and plates,

her taste buds,
and her zeal for life
when you left.

i should have savoured
the taste of every moment
while our home was still filled with life.

when you left,
i buried our love
in a casket
built from insecurity and hopelessness.
i still hoard your love
and our memories,
even the bad ones.

because of you,
i believe in good men
but fear that every man i might love
will come as you came—
gentle, loving, kind, patient, and warm,
then grow into a moody, vile, violent, and cold stranger.

when exactly did the peace of God escape you?
when did the shadow of your body
become a violent brute?

i miss you,
the old you.

Far Away

your mere existence
even though it unfolded at a distance,
kept my teenage memories with you alive.

Second Chances

even when people hurt you,
they are supposed to go on living...

what am i supposed to do with all this grief now?

Going Back Home

i wish i could go back home
go back in time
to when you were still around
just to bask in the warmth of your love
one last time

kuyabanda la ngikhona kubuhlungu

EX

An ex is an ugly thing.

A living, walking, tormenting past.

A lover who has changed form and now repulses you.

Poems I Wrote For You While You Were Gone

I hate you!
I hate you!
I hate you!

Please stay...

You
Remind
Me
Of
My Past

At least you've returned,
Now carrying pieces of my father.

Okuhle Esethu

"I Love You"

Do not throw "I love you"
as if you were playfully casting a stone into a river.
Even the smallest stone can create ripples
that will rip this heart into rags.

Dear Love

you have disappointed me,
again!

Heartbreak

the most harmful way to grieve
after a heartbreak
is to be in denial,
to self-gaslight,
feeling stupid for feeling.

Healing Bruises

when you get bruised,
you need to sit in your pain,
allow yourself to go through the emotions.

you can't rush the healing process.
you can't force yourself to be happy.
you can't erase all the memories
when your body is dense with melancholy.

How To Deal With A Heartbreak

1. Grieve.

2. Feel the heaviness of your emotions.

3. Cry about it.

4. Conjure up old memories, revisit the past.

5. Mourn the parts of yourself you lost loving them.

Experiences

my mother tells me that everything has a lifespan.

holding onto our eroding friendship
felt like gripping
a rugged rope that tore my skin to tatters.

the end of our friendship
was a gruesome and gory festival.
i mourned it before it even decayed,
watching our bond slowly lose its tang,
like the toasted bread you always left to dry up
when your mood swings clogged your appetite.

the love we shared
left a bitter taste in my mouth,
like the lemons we would suck
after drowning our mojitos on friday nights.

the joyous sound of our raucous laughter,
rattling against walls,
rings torturously in my brain.

Okuhle Esethu

i cannot erase the beautiful images
of our swaying, energetic bodies,
heightening the vibrancy of silent rooms.

you are an experience
my imagination revisits when life feels dull.

Tug-Of-War

my heart   and   my mind

have been playing

tug-of-war

letting go…   …holding on

Scattered Iterations Of Life

memories
have neither a beginning nor an end

memories
exist outside of time

memories
change a little each time we revisit them

                                        i am forgetting your face

The Past

we collected memories
in place of tombstones.

remembering became tiresome.
forgetting was a chore,
more burdensome.

so, we lingered between
remembering and forgetting,
letting go and holding on,
life and death...

A Heavenly Letter

Dear Sibling,

Mama just told me she lost you
before I could even meet you.

I wonder what you would have looked like,
or how strong our bond would have been.

I am lonely as an only child.
Do you know me?

Am I a sister to you?
Or a stranger you nearly crossed paths with?

I am sorry I did not weep or mourn for you
when you did not make it home.

I did not even know that you were coming.

Mourning Shadows

Don't beat yourself up
when mourning loved ones
from the past makes you angry.

Don't be angry
when you forget their faces.

Remembering is work!
When you are bereaved,
you will have limited strength.

You will only have energy to stretch one arm
to snooze your alarm
in the morning.

You will only have energy to open your eyes
and stare at the ceiling for hours
later in the day.

Okuhle Esethu

When you are grieving,
save your energy for the trivial things
that will keep you alive.

Remembering might kill you!

Mourning shadows of memories
is easier than
mourning vivid faces you will never see again.

Uninvited Visitor

You inflict pain.
You are the reason families feud.
You take and never give back.
How selfish are you!?
Abo mama abafelokazi.
Izingane izintandane.

Precursor of anger, hate,
famine, feuds, and fear,
frustration, depression, and confusion.

There is nothing positive about you.
Not that I am perfect,
I know you are coming for me too.

You are a homewrecker.
You are a thief
of joy, peace, and hope.

Childhood Museum

Gogo's Home
is not just a house that shelters us.
It is a kraal of love that makes us, us.
It is a storage house for our hopes and dreams.
It is a distinct regathering of dissipating
childhood memories.

Every time we revisit that museum,
the past swells our grieving bodies with love.

Keep that home alive!

Home

We know this land better than anyone else.
We were raised here from birth.

This land knows each of us
by name and by birthmark.
The soil can tell which strides
belong to whose feet
and which women are about to give birth.
The trees have given us life
and taught us of the abundance of life.
The grass and stones have conjured tales
that kept us entertained as children.

This is our fortress!
With high, insurmountable walls
made from sticks and stones,
where we bury our secrets and bones.
The gates have ears but never judge us.

Okuhle Esethu

You can claim ownership of this land
on paper,
but it will never be yours.
It will never love you like it has loved us.

You cannot erase our memories.
You cannot unmake our history.
You will never destroy our bond
with OUR HOME!

The Bygone Days

Gone are the days
when Gogo's Home was still Gogo's Home—
homely, warm, forever filled with
the strong aroma of vanilla essence.
A place for joyful memories and family reunions.
A well of love and laughter.

Now,
it's just a house,
laden with war and resentment.

A museum
congested with distant memories
of a childhood that was once precious.

Gone are the days
when life was kinder,
my family closer,
our bond stronger.

Death And Disease

We are here.
We are still here.
Ikusasa alithembisi kodwa sisese lapha.

A nation strangled and suffocated in its own corset.
Persons, priests, professors, and presidents
plagued by helplessness.

A human race jolted out of reality
by disease, destruction, and doom.
Experiencing life as a mere audience in our own story.

We have no control.
But we are still here!

Qhawe

when a GIANT falls,
the voices and souls
of the children of the soil
tremble in grief, anxiety, and sorrow.
another legend lost. another may soon follow.

***Qhawe- A legend.

The Culture

In the heart of Braam,
the face of a traumatised youth fills the streets.
Their eyes are pooled with tears.
Their hearts heavy with grief mixed with gratitude.
Their ecstasy turned into ash.

Everything he does and did, they wanna do.
They multiply, and their culture never dies.
Their light, called Riky, dies
a mere heartbeat away from his home.
The place he made his music in becomes his coffin.

Culture is human. Culture is not perfect.
They lay him to rest and bury the parts of culture
that killed him and kills them.
The parts of culture that makes them
hate themselves, life, others, and the culture itself.

His music mimicked God's face and form.
His thundering presence uplifted the youth.
His heart held the entire world in awe.

An extension of God's love, now reunited with God.
uBaba ufuna azom'thuma
so the stars die young.
They disappear into a warm darkness
and leave the world brighter than they found it.
uBaba ufuna azom'thuma.

Okuhle Esethu

Goodbye for keeps

How can a being
once swelled with life
become a body of granite stone?

Death carves irreparable holes in our hearts,
forcing us to live
without those who gave us life.

We live on
with unutterable pain in our bodies,
making death the mistress of our existence.

Friend

For Mashudu Tshamano

Thank you
for being there,
in silence,
with no words of comfort,
while my sobs of grief
lingered heavily in the sorrow-filled air.

Thank you for being a friend.

Living With Grief

You miss it sometimes, you know.
Once you've healed, you miss it.

What?

The pain.

You miss it when it's gone.
When it's all you've known,
you become comfortable living with it.

It becomes your best friend.
It keeps you up at night.
It creeps up in conversations
and tortures you for attention
during the day.

And when it finally leaves,
you realise you are nothing without it;
you can't define yourself outside of it.

WOMANING

PART 3: WOMANING

1. The Moon.
2. Mother's Sacrifice.
3. SHE.
4. The Art of Seduction.
5. Love Says.
6. Desire.
7. Loved.
8. Loving Parents.
9. Courtship.
10. And God Said.
11. Living In Fear.
12. Do Not Ask Girls If They Are Virgins.
13. My Silence Was My Healing.
14. Your Body.
15. This Is!
16. The Spells of Puberty.
17. Day 28.
18. 18 Years Living.
19. Being A Woman.
20. The Shocks of Womanhood.
21. Womaning…

Ugh, I'm Only 21!

Mother

SHE

Femininity

Love

Self-Worth

Courtship

Misogyny

Patriarchy

Trauma

Healing

My Body

Puberty

Virginity

Silence

Womanhood

The Moon

In the sky,
the moon is round,
beautiful, perfect, holy.
Nothing like mother,
who wears a disguise for my eyes only.

Hiding her softness
behind her roughness.
Mother is nothing like the moon.

Mother is
the moon, the sky, the stars.
Mother is not perfect.
Mother is heavenly.

Okuhle Esethu

Mother's Sacrifice

See how hollow i've become.
An empty body with fleeting dreams,
emptying herself,
bearing her soul to the world.

To be seen.
To be a vessel of God's purpose,
a vessel of healing,
a vessel of hope for the unseen.

i cannot unsee the emptiness
in my mother's voice
when she spoke of dreams unfulfilled.

i cannot erase the density of the brokenness
and courage that lined her facade
when she gave up on her dreams
to make space for me and my dreams.

SHE

When she escaped her mother's womb,
she inhaled the earthly energy
and exhaled her ethereality
into the world.
Each breath of hers carried with it divinity.

Her presence
made the heavens weep,
the angels dance,
and the stars worship her.

A WOMAN
is a nectar of life,
embodying boundless wisdom
that crosses into infinity.

Her scars are her stars.
She rises and shines bright
even when battered and bruised,
burdened with the weight of womanhood
by our unjust society.

Okuhle Esethu

Her dreams and aspirations
are often buried
under the cruel soils of patriarchy.

But when you bury a seed,
expect it to grow into a tree of greatness
and nourishment.

An extension of God's love.
She is light
piercing through the darkness of misogyny.

A WOMAN.
The voice of other voices.
Her tongue is like a sword
that slices through the downgrading lies
told about women.

Making words bleed,
she rewrites history,
reshapes society,
and forces the world to take heed.

When you see a woman,
know that she does not stand alone;
God braided strength into her skin.
She gives her life and power to her next of kin.
She carries the strength
of the women before her
and the women after her
inside her.

A WOMAN
with power no man can seize,
the troubles and traumas
society bestows upon her
are stones she uses to step into her greatness.

She stands against all waves of sexism,
gender inequality, and patriarchy,
and braves the belly of the beast
with blazing fire in her belly.

A WOMAN
is
a gold mine of intelligence,
a heavenly breed, the closest thing to God.

Okuhle Esethu

The Art of Seduction

To seduce a man,
look at the moon.

Ravishing and rare,
she causes all men to stare.

She moves with calm stillness:
slowly, serenely, silently.

Enveloped with grace that overcomes darkness.
Exudes gentleness with a dash of hardness.

She appears only once
but has a powerful presence.

An unfamiliar face that seduces priests into sinners
and commands worship from wild, hairy beasts.

Angelic in nature.
Pure in appearance.

To seduce a man,
act like the moon.

Love Says

This love says
I am not worthy of it.
I am too this and not that for it.
It wants me to prove myself worthy of it,
to worship and bow to it,
to lose myself in it.

This love is a liar.

I believe in the love that
accepts me as I am
and still makes me want to be better.

Love that loves me with my flaws and insecurities.
Love that has no shape or form.
Love that is pure but has its imperfections.
Love that is sacred but non-judgemental.
Love that makes me feel safe, wanted, and loved.
Love that sees me.
Love that respects me.

Desire

I want love
that feels like the rich smell of cinnamon
whipping my nostrils when I walk into my Gogo's kitchen.
Love that is warm and feels like home.

I want love
that feels like my baby sister's hugs.
Love that is safe and trustworthy,
ready to catch me whenever I fall into its arms.

I want old love,
like my mother's R&B playlist.
Love that is slow and gentle,
assuring, and sure of itself.

I want love
that is as consistent as
bank notifications and phone calls from my father.

Love that is not fickle.
Love that does not make me overthink.
Love that does not make me feel insecure.
That's the kind of love I deserve.

Loved

I want to be clothed with love and security.
I want to be held like an egg about to hatch.
I want to be treated like a princess.

Loving Parents

You were born into a loving home.

You've learned that love has a face
a body
a voice
a soul
a heart
a rhythm
a beat and a heartbeat.

You've learned that love
looks like your nurturing mother,
sounds like your protective father.
It is safe and accepting of you,
like the home you grew up in.

You've learned that love is supposed to
nurture
care
protect
feed
and tickle you
the way your parents did when you were a child.

Okuhle Esethu

You are grown now; you've learned.

You've learned what love
looks
feels
and sounds like.

So, why do you search for love
in unfamiliar faces?

Why do you search for love
in strangers with bodies
clogged with hate and abandonment?

Where did you learn to love this love
that does not even come close
to loving you the way your parents did?

Courtship

potential suitors dance around my body,
attempting to hold onto my booty,
to arrest me with their fogs of masculinity.

i read their energy;
it exudes misogyny,
so, i dance away.

instead of swaying away
when they can't get their way,
they force their way.

Okuhle Esethu

And God Said

One day,
God created a woman,
then God created a man
from the woman's womb.

A man with no scruples
who saw the woman's garden
and decided that it would be his to own,
to plow whenever he liked,
to sow seeds of his unmanliness,
then harvest fruits of her womanhood.

God said,
"This woman shall give life.
The man shall honour her life
and depend on her for his life."

The man rewrote God's rule of life
by trying to rule over her life.

Living In Fear

My fear
is not that he will make me beg for my life,
then rape me
before decorating the streets
with my red-stained, lifeless body.

My fear
is not that my friends and family will be left
drowning in grief, torture, trauma, and turmoil
when the news reaches them.

My fear
is that he will kill me before my time
and bury me with my dreams.
He will seize the pen from my gifted hands
and rewrite my story as if he were my God.

My fear
is that he will forcibly redefine my destiny
and make everyone remember me
as the girl who died at the hands of another man,
not the girl who touched lives and inspired many.

Okuhle Esethu

I won't be remembered
the way I want to be remembered
because of him.
I'll be mourned, not celebrated.
My obituary will be bloodied and too short.

My fear
is that I will take my last breath
wrestling his vicious hands and wan body
before I even get to see my dreams materialise.

My fear
is that I will die a victim, too.

Do Not Ask Girls If They Are Virgins

Do not ask girls if they are virgins.

For us girls,
our first time
is never really our first time.

Men usually decide when it is our time
before we even discover our bodies.

They maze around our forming thighs,
in search of our unripe fruits,
and steal from our gardens
with drooling tongues
and hungry teeth
before our bosoms bloom and our breasts burst.

They turn our unknowing bodies
into unexplored landscapes of pleasure,
casting us into roles that we do not belong in,
treating our bodies as decorations
to charm their sinister manhood.

Okuhle Esethu

Do not ask girls if they are virgins.

Do not ask girls if anyone has broken their virginity.
A man's dick has no power
to break a woman's body,
even though men often break into our bodies.

Sometimes it's the boy we like,
the guy from the spaza shop, the geography teacher,
the old retired next-door neighbour, the preacher,
the Uber driver, or even the beloved uncle.

Do not ask girls if they are virgins.

Men and our patriarchal society
whisper to us that a woman
who knows her way
around her own body
is insolent and unmarriageable.

For us girls,
our first time
is when we choose to defy
those oppressive myths about sex and pleasure.

For us girls,

when we say

our first time,

we are usually referring to

when we finally discover our bodies

and reclaim ownership over them,

embracing that our bodies belong to us,

not men or an oppressive society.

For us girls,

our first time

is when we untangle the complexities of sexuality,

pluck the stigmas of sex

that were once planted inside our minds

with seeds of shame and fear,

and shatter the lies told to us

about what makes a decent woman.

For us girls,

our first time

is when we break free

from the shackles of the myth of female virginity,

which oppresses us and hinders us

from loving and exploring our bodies,

dictating that we ought to wait for incapable men
to discover our bodies
for us.

For us girls,
our first time
is when we decide to willingly share
our bodies with others,
inviting them inside us,
with consent, not coercion,
knowing that sex does not make a woman
less of a woman.
Sex and pleasure
are part of the feminine experience.

For us girls,
our first time
is when we liberate ourselves,
have sex because we want to
and when our bodies ask us to.

Do not ask girls if they are still virgins.

Do not ask girls if anyone has broken their virginity,

because as a girl,

how do you tell someone

that you are having sex for the first time

but have had a man maze

around your unknowing body before?

Do not ask girls if they are still virgins.

Okuhle Esethu

My Silence Was My Healing

My silence has been the strongest part of me.

It knows and understands me
better than the loud parts of myself.

It has helped me conceal myself
from this crude world and my cruel self.

When I was suffocating
with brutal memories and conflicting thoughts,
it taught me how to breathe again.

It held my hand and reassured me
that it believed me.

It stayed when I was bleeding
and guided me through the labyrinth of hurt.

It kept me warm
when my heart was ice-cold with hatred.

Ugh,Life!

It kept me sane
and restrained me from slitting my wrists
when my body was fraught with pain,
my thighs swelled with trauma,
my mind blank with uncertainty.

It was my strength and solace
when things were falling apart
faster than I could put them together.

My silence was my healing
when I could not trust the world
with my fragile truth.

Your Body

when you have conversations about
your body
and recount your experiences
with it,

his name
might creep in,
the way he sneaked around your thighs
when no one was watching,

and
accidentally
slip from the tip of your tongue.

that
does not mean he owns
your body.

you are free
from his possessive nature now,

                                                   but still healing.

This Is!

Dear men,

This is
Not yours
To claim or possess.

This is
My Body My Body My Body My Body My Body My Body
My Body My Body My Body My Body My Body My Body
My Body My Body My Body My Body My Body My Body
My Body My Body My Body My Body My Body My Body
My Body My Body My Body My Body My Body My Body
My Body My Body My Body My Body My Body My Body
My Body My Body My Body My Body My Body My Body
My Body My Body My Body My Body My Body My Body
My Body My Body My Body My Body My Body My Body
My Body My Body My Body My Body My Body My Body
My Body My Body My Body My Body My Body My Body
My Body My Body My Body My Body My Body My Body
My Body My Body My Body My Body My Body My Body

Okuhle Esethu

My Body My Body My Body My Body My Body My Body
My Body My Body My Body My Body My Body My Body
My Body My Body My Body My Body My Body My Body
My Body My Body My Body My Body My Body My Body
My Body My Body My Body My Body My Body My Body
My Body My Body My Body My Body My Body My Body
My Body My Body My Body My Body My Body My Body
My Body My Body My Body My Body My Body My Body
My Body My Body My Body My Body My Body My Body
My Body My Body My Body My Body My Body My Body
My Body My Body My Body My Body My Body My Body
My Body My Body My Body My Body My Body My Body
My Body My Body My Body My Body My Body My Body
My Body My Body My Body My Body My Body My Body
My Body My Body My Body My Body My Body My Body
My Body My Body My Body My Body My Body My Body
My Body My Body My Body My Body My Body My Body
My Body My Body My Body My Body My Body My Body
My Body My Body My Body My Body My Body My Body
My Body My Body My Body My Body My Body My Body
My Body My Body My Body My Body My Body My Body
My Body My Body My Body My Body My Body My Body
My Body My Body My Body My Body My Body My Body
My Body My Body My Body My Body My Body My Body
My Body My Body My Body My Body My Body My Body

Ugh,Life!

My Body My Body My Body My Body My Body My Body
My Body My Body My Body My Body My Body My Body
My Body My Body My Body My Body My Body My Body
My Body My Body My Body My Body My Body My Body
My Body My Body My Body My Body My Body My Body
My Body My Body My Body My Body My Body My Body
My Body My Body My Body My Body My Body My Body
My Body My Body My Body My Body My Body My Body
My Body My Body My Body My Body My Body My Body
My Body My Body My Body My Body My Body My Body
My Body My Body My Body My Body My Body My Body
My Body My Body My Body My Body My Body My Body
My Body My Body My Body My Body My Body My Body
My Body My Body My Body My Body My Body My Body
My Body My Body My Body My Body My Body My Body
My Body My Body My Body My Body My Body My Body
My Body My Body My Body My Body My Body My Body
My Body My Body My Body My Body My Body My Body
My Body My Body My Body My Body My Body My Body
My Body My Body My Body My Body My Body My Body
My Body My Body My Body My Body My Body My Body
My Body My Body My Body My Body My Body My Body
My Body My Body My Body My Body My Body My Body
My Body My Body My Body My Body My Body!

The Spells of Puberty

Alas!
The spells of puberty
have hooked themselves onto me.

My body develops in and out of shape.
My breasts pop out of my chest like grape.
The cushions under my vagina force me
to walk like an ape.
I overindulge in food and watch my weight fluctuate.

I am a fledging woman
with the claws of adolescence digging into my skin.
Subtle fat takes over my body and builds itself a home.
My brothers don't look at me the same;
they drool like dogs when I go home.

I bulge and become insecure.
My body and I are strangers at war.
Mirrors don't reflect the body I asked God for.
The unfamiliarity leaves me with a new scar.

18 Years Living

I've lived in this body
for 18 years.

It has felt both like hell and home.
Together, my body and I
have fought wars unbeknownst to the world,
overcome insecurities
and pandemics like depression.

I've lived in this body
for 18 years.

It has felt like a familiar land
and a foreign asylum.
Together, my body and I
have survived inner attacks
and words as sharp as swords
from outsiders with displaced stares.

I've lived in this body
for 18 years.

Okuhle Esethu

It has felt like floating on self-acceptance
and drowning in shallow swamps of self-doubt.
Together, my body and I
have inhaled self-love
and exhaled self-hatred.

This body
My body
has been a fountainhead for streams
that divide into low self-esteem at times
and confidence that is often confused for cockiness.

Together, my body and I
have created magic,
dreamed and evolved,
learned to love and live life wholeheartedly.

Together, my body and I
have learned to be patient with one another
as we grow into unfamiliar shapes
with each year that passes.

I've lived in this body
for 18 years.

Being A Woman

Ugh, this hair!

It gives me backaches
when I let it down for too long.

So, I tie it up into a bun,
only for it to be heavy on my neck instead.

The Shocks of Womanhood

It enters all at once,
without warning,
without even asking for your permission.

And no one ever prepares you for its heaviness.

Womaning

when she ceases to rage at the world,
the storm brews silently inside her,
fanning her flames of trauma.

her body becomes a battlefield
as she struggles
for survival.

...

About The Author

Okuhle Esethu, legally known as Lindokuhle Esethu Hlatshwayo, is a South African writer, poet, performer, and literature enthusiast with an undying passion for storytelling. She is also a B.A. alumnus of the University of Johannesburg, where she double majored in English Literature and Film Studies. She graduated cum laude and received an award for the most innovative screenplay at the third-year level.